The Week

by Mary Lindeen • illustrated by Javier González

Content Consultant: Susan Kesselring, M.A., Literacy Educator and Preschool Director

visit us at

www.abdopublishing.com

Published by Magic Wagon, a division of the ABDO Publishing Group, 8000 West 78th Street, Edina, Minnesota, 55439. Copyright © 2008 by Abdo Consulting Group, Inc. International copyrights reserved in all countries. All rights reserved. No part of this book may be reproduced in any form without written permission from the publisher. Looking Glass Library™ is a trademark and logo of Magic Wagon.

Printed in the United States.

Text by Mary Lindeen
Illustrations by Javier González
Edited by Patricia Stockland
Interior layout and design by Becky Daum
Cover design by Becky Daum

Library of Congress Cataloging-in-Publication Data

Lindeen, Mary.
  The week / Mary Lindeen ; illustrated by Javier A. González ; content consultant, Susan Kesselring.
     p. cm. —— (Days of the week)
  ISBN 978-1-60270-103-8
  1. Days—Juvenile literature. 2. Week—Juvenile literature. I. González, Javier A., 1974- ill. II. Kesselring, Susan.
III. Title.
  GR930.L569 2008
  529'.1—dc22
                    2007034080

The seven days in a week
are always the same.
Do you know what they are?
Let's say all the names.

Sunday, Monday, Tuesday,

Wednesday, Thursday,

Friday, Saturday.

You knew those big words!

Hip, hip, hooray!

Put these days in a row

and then tell me fast,

which days make the weekend?

Yes, the first and the last.

OK, look again

and answer this riddle,

do you know what we call

the five days in the middle?

All the Mondays through Fridays,

these are the weekdays,

the go-to-school,

come home,

and play hide-and-seek days.

Seven days in this order,

we call them a week.

Fifty-two weeks are a year.

What? Count them all? Eek!

Some days of the week

are not to be missed.

They are known as holidays.

Don't forget them. Make a list!

Whether weekday or weekend,

whether holiday or not,

here are some things

that each day has got.

_____

Every day has two 12 o'clocks—
at midnight and at noon—
and a dawn and a dusk.
Greet the sun! Greet the moon!

Yesterday is the day
just over and done.
Tomorrow's on its way
and filled with more fun.
So no matter which day
of the week you are in,
fill it with giggles
and plenty of grins.

The Days of the Week

1
Sunday

2
Monday

3
Tuesday

7 Saturday

5 Thursday

6 Friday

4 Wednesday

COUNTING DOWN THE DAYS IN A WEEK

Make a paper chain that has seven loops of paper linked together. Use two different colors of paper: one color for the first and last links (the weekend), the second color for the five links in the middle (the weekdays). Beginning on a Sunday, tear off one link on the chain each night before you go to bed. When you tear off the last link, you are done with the week!

CREATE YOUR OWN DAYS

Now it's your turn to name the days of the week! Pretend that you have been hired to come up with new names for each day of the week. What are the seven new names that you would choose? How did you think of those?

WORDS TO KNOW

dawn: the beginning of the day, when the sun is rising.

dusk: after the sun sets and before the night arrives, when it is almost dark.

holiday: a special festival or celebration day, when people don't go to work or school as they usually would do.

midnight: twelve o'clock in the middle of the night.

noon: twelve o'clock in the middle of the day.

tomorrow: the day after today.

weekday: any day of the week except Saturday or Sunday.

weekend: the days at the beginning and end of the week; Saturday and Sunday.

yesterday: the day before today.